No More BOYFRIENDS

The Strategies and Detours of A Committed Relationship

KATRINA MARIE CURTIS

© 2019 by Katrina Marie Curtis
No More Boyfriends: The Strategies and Detours of A Committed Relationship

Published by 13th & Joan

All rights reserved. No part of this publication may be reproduced, distributed, or transmitted in any form or by any means, including photocopying, recording, or other electronic or mechanical methods, without the prior written permission of the publisher, except in the case of brief quotations embodied in critical reviews and certain other noncommercial uses permitted by copyright law. For permission requests, write to the publisher, addressed "Attention: Permissions Coordinator," at the address below.

13th & Joan
500 N. Michigan Avenue, Suite #600
Chicago, IL 60611
WWW.13THANDJOAN.COM

Ordering Information:
13th & Joan books may be purchased for educational, business or sales promotional use. For information, please email the Sales Department at sales@13thandjoan.com.

Author Photograph by Ballie B. Photography

Printed in the United States of America

ISBN: 978-1-7331313-8-4

Publisher's Cataloging-in-Publication data has been applied for.

First Edition Printed, March 2019
Library of Congress Cataloging-in-Publication Data has been applied for.

First Edition

10 9 8 7 6 5 4 3 2 1

Dedication

THIS BOOK IS dedicated to my daughters, McKenzie and Micah. I've seen and experienced so much unnecessary hurt and pain due to navigating blindly from relationship to relationship trying to figure out how to get the right one. I had no one to tell me how valuable I am, no one to express to me what a healthy relationship looks like, and no one to express to me that I am worth the work it takes to be with me and not to settle for anything less than the value I offer. THIS is the very thing I want my daughters to understand before they date, as they are dating, and when they marry. YOU are worthy of the man who is committed to bringing joy to you and experiencing joy with you. And how YOU see and value YOURSELF will be the determining factor of what you get. Be INTENTIONAL as well as ACCOUNTABLE. MOMMA'S GOT YO BACK!

Foreword

FIRST AND FOREMOST, I wanna (yes, wanna) thank God who has been my sustainer through ALL things. I realize that this book was less about me and more about ministry. God has guided me through many heartbreaks and allowed me to learn lessons to break not only the generational relationship curses of women, but to be the transparent example of what ACCOUNTABILITY to oneself looks like. I thank Him for not hardening my heart through all that I have experienced so that I can still give women hope. The love that women desire does exist, despite all the noise of this bitter and broken world. Who says that it doesn't?

Acknowledgments

I HAVE TO ACKNOWLEDGE the one woman who gave me a HUGE voice without knowing that she did: my mom, Mary Cheirs. She provided me with every activity and opportunity she could to grow my confidence in a time where being a little chocolate girl with a gap in her teeth (yep … I had a gap, y'all) was not popular, much less beautiful. From dance classes to Girl Scouts, 4-H public speaking and singing solos in the choir, you made me understand that I added just as much value as anyone else to any situation I involved myself in. And for that, I will forever be grateful. I love you beyond myself.

There are three people who were really consistent in believing in me through the whole "No More Boyfriends" movement and book from day one.

No More Boyfriends

Que Jackson: Thank you for being my unofficial everything when it comes to putting me in the eyes and ears of the right people. Our friendship is special and necessary. When I didn't feel like I could keep going, you made me stretch myself. I am so appreciative for you.

Crystal "Crissy" Patton: You believed in me soooo much and would do without me even asking. I remember you telling me that you got me. You were ALWAYS there and you BELIEVED in me to the point that you did the work and asked nothing in return. You shared my posts and watched my videos. You told people how dope I was. You did footwork and made me confident that what I was doing was the right thing! You believed me so much that you went out and got you a husband that same year! LOL! I love you beyond words.

To my bestie, Danielle Hood: Your gift was different. You were my friend when I had nothing, when I was still unfamiliar in most people's ear. When I cried because people betrayed me, love had let me down, and I was unsure of what was next, you were there to comfort me, let me cuss, and let me vent without judging me. We have a

Katrina Marie Curtis

friendship that I will never take for granted. And I love you to the moon and back.

Thank you Ardre Orie and 13th & Joan Publishing House for believing in me and giving me a permanent voice to impact the way women contribute to and control their relationship success. It's all on you, Boo! #Ding!

Preface
TO HAVE A BOYFRIEND OR NOT HAVE A BOYFRIEND? THAT IS THE QUESTION.

THE QUESTION OF whether or not we should have a boyfriend has plagued me for quite some time. I was drawn to conduct some research on this concept from another perspective. A boyfriend is defined as a male friend or acquaintance with whom one is platonically, romantically, or sexually involved. The most intriguing aspect of the definition is that it was associated with short-term connections. Words like husband and partner were used to describe relationships that are assumed to span for longer periods of time and, even more startling, committed relationships. So, does this mean that a boyfriend is assumed to be a short-term relationship that we should expect very little commitment from? If so, then I must ask ... Is this what we are looking for ladies?

As I see it, why must we even accept the term *boyfriend* when you have a husband expectations? In the intro of an article I read on *Black and Married with Kids*: "3 Wifely Duties and Husbandly Tasks That Keep Your Home Running Smoothly" it stated:

Girlfriend duties to wifely duties [and boyfriend duties to husbandly duties]–with the change in relationship status comes a change in duties and tasks ... Responsibilities and expectations change as well; and for each household, it is different. Your mate will not have the same expectation of you or you of them, as your neighbor has of their mate. It's personal. It's something that needs ... communication. If not, the expectation will be unmet and you will end up with two unhappy people. Tell the truth: You do not expect the same thing of a boyfriend as you do of a husband or vice versa. When you say, "I do," things change—They increase for the better.

Katrina Marie Curtis

This excerpt helps me sum up what I've been saying. In the boyfriend stage (which I choose to call the intentional stage) there should be no wifely duties given or husbandly duties received.

A man that wants to be a husband will provide the platform for growth without accepting anything he doesn't want to give back in return.

The exchange of power will EMPOWER the both of you to transition to the PURPOSED couple you were created to be.

Men are so offended by the idea of self help or self growth when it comes to women because they feel like it's an attack against them. Some feel that the suggestion only comes out of anger when something goes wrong … But isn't that where most healthy lifestyle and habits are birthed? Out of hurt or tragedy?

My goal is for women to be proactive not reactive. It's easier to eat healthy and exercise from the beginning than to try to lose the weight later. Detoxing from an addiction is hella hard. Not impossible, but just unnecessary.

Table of Contents

Preface: To have a boyfriend or not have a boyfriend? That is the Question. xi

Introduction: This One is for My Ladies 1

1. Preparing for the Task 3
2. Knowing What You Want 9
3. Meeting 17
4. Why Are Men Offended by Women Empowerment? 27
5. Keeping the Pace 33
6. Stages, Not Titles 37
7. Prove What to Who? 41
8. Why Does He Want to Be With You? 45
9. Chess, Not Checkers 49
10. Intention vs. Intentional 53
11. Detour 59

12. Love Language 63

13. Expectations and Credentials................................67

14. Types of Men to Avoid..71

Bonus: Let's Talk About Sex 79

P.S..83

Outro..91

Say What! Quotes Worth Keeping From *No More Boyfriends* 95

About T. Marie.. 103

Connect with T. Marie... 107

Introduction
THIS ONE IS FOR MY LADIES

Ladies. Ladies. Ladies.

Allow me to ask you a question. If someone could potentially teach you how to avoid having your heart broken, would you be willing to listen? Life, love, and even loss has taught me so many valuable lessons about what *not* to do in the dating arena that I would be remiss to keep all of this tea (as we call it in the south) to myself. They say that if it doesn't kill you, it makes you stronger. Well here I am, still standing in the name of love.

Through it all, the greatest lesson I gleaned was about loving myself. Like you, I've heard it said so many times that "You must love yourself first," but looking back, I struggled to do so while actively searching for love. Today, I recognize that women need more than a point in the right direction. We are desperately in need of real-life strategies and conversations to navigate the dating waters. The purpose of this book is not meant to weigh you down with reading, but to call your attention to some grossly important details to consider when you know with the fullness of your heart that you are ready for love. And even if you are not there yet, this book will help you take care of you first. Trust me, you deserve the very best of what life and love have to offer. Everything that your heart desires is out there, but it can't find it's way to you until you've done the work to find yourself.

PREPARING FOR THE TASK

one

My last relationship taught Before dating, get yourself together.
—T. Marie

DATING IS INDEED a task and not something that you just fall into. Taking time to listen to your heart before engaging in the dating game is necessary. Are you healing? Carrying baggage? Are you using the dating game as a Band-Aid? If so, you will have a hard time succeeding in the next committed relationship. There are times when you need the pain of being alone and loss to go away first. Love can hurt like hell. The hard truth is that

No More Boyfriends

when you date in this space, you unknowingly transfer feelings that could be toxic to the innocent bystander. Operating in this capacity is like getting drunk to ease the pain. After you become sober, you recognize that you have involved another person in your unresolved emotions. This is dangerous for so many reasons because the other person who was unsuspecting, with potential hopes of a good relationship, is damaged in the process. Much like a drunk driver, you have engaged in a hit and run incident. Dating in this capacity can also mean that you have the power to hurt someone who had no idea you were coming. It's true … hurt people, hurt people. Get yourself to the point of wholeness before you bring another person into your life. You deserve better, and their heart deserves your consideration.

Preparing for a relationship or marriage should also mean healing from past relationships and past hurt, defining happiness on your own terms, recognizing self-esteem triggers, and learning to love the woman you see in the mirror. It is also imperative that you resolve to work on anything that hinders you from feeling worthy. You've likely heard it before, but nothing could be more true: Healing can only take place when you learn how to fall in love with yourself first. An integral part of the healing process is taking time to understand what happened in your past failed relationships, and what part you played in it. I wish that someone had told me how to get over regret. I had no idea how much of a role it had the power to play, and I carried it with me, which also meant that it was transferred in relationships. You must work through it. You deserve to be in a good space when preparing to enter the dating game and discover love. Not making peace with regret also means accepting baggage. The baggage that I speak of can weigh you down in ways unimaginable. You can't carry such a heavy burden while trying to move forward. Baggage has the power to slow you down and even bring you to your breaking point if you allow it. Spend time alone learning who you really are and what you truly desire from life and partnership. Time alone can reveal things about yourself that you had not otherwise known. Sitting in silence and peace allows you to hear from yourself. You would be surprised by the things that you didn't really know about yourself because of being around others or in a relationship constantly. When you are by yourself, you learn so much about your perspective on life. If you don't like being with you, how can you expect someone else to want to be with you?

It is imperative that you recognize how past hurt has affected you and heal from it so that you have the power to avoid taking this baggage into your future relationships. You deserve better.

7 ACTIONS EVERY WOMAN MUST TAKE BEFORE DATING

1. **Take Back Me Time:** You need alone time, and time to heal. You deserve time to find out who you are and time to learn to appreciate yourself.

2. **Talk to Successful Couples:** Gain perspective on what healthy relationships and love looks like and allow yourself to witness successful relationships.

3. **Be Aware of your Ideal Relationship:** You need to know what you want and what you're looking for.

4. **Be Content With Who You Are:** Be certain that you're not looking for missing things in other people. You need and deserve to have a sense of completeness.

5. **Get A Life:** Stay busy and be comfortable in your routine so that you are okay with or without a relationship. You need to have interests outside of men. Your significant other should not be your complete life.

6. **Ask God/Universe:** Conversation with God, or the universe, for guidance and direction for your path is necessary. Exercise discernment, and trust your instincts and intuition.

7. **Get Your Self-Esteem Together:** You have to be confident in who you are and know your worth. Know that you deserve better than a man who just wants to use you. Stay confident in who you are and what you have to offer the world.

two

KNOWING WHAT YOU WANT

*There is no crime
in wanting something
meaningful from
a relationship.
—T. Marie*

WHEN IT COMES to relationships, you have to know what it is your heart desires. It's okay to just want something casual. It is also okay to desire a deeper connection. Either way, you must never forget that the choice is yours. Most importantly, you must be truthful with yourself. If you are just looking to pass time with some select company, don't judge yourself for acting accordingly. The key is not to trick yourself into believing that you want something far less than what you deserve. It is equally important that you connect with like minds. You cannot desire "Happily Ever After" and connect with someone who just wants a temporary acquaintance. We have a tendency to think that we can change the minds and hearts of people by being Mrs. Right. Far too often, we believe that doing all the right things, making all the right moves, and showing someone what love looks like (even when they're not looking for love) will result in a fairytale romance. This is an unrealistic pattern of thinking and most often results in heartbreak. In theory, it doesn't make sense. How can we be moved to anger and place blame on the other person when WE have served as the biggest factor in wasting our time based on unclear or unrealistic expectations? This is not to take away the responsibility of those that you may have felt used by, and those that made their intentions unclear, but you must call your attention to the power that YOU have and the choices that YOU make. Ultimately, you are responsible for yourself. When you realize your worth, you will also be led to invest your time wisely.

To decide what you want from a relationship, first identify what your core needs are. All of your decisions should be based upon what you need and how you can contribute to the empowerment of another. Eliminate people, places, and things that make you sacrifice yourself. Surround yourself with people, places, and things that complement you and your divine purpose. Closely examine your friendships and relationships, and pay close attention to who you are most happy being around.

Casual dating can be a way to find out what you desire. One consideration during this phase is dating without sexual intimacy. Engaging in this way can help you learn a great deal about yourself and the person with whom you've connected. Sexual intimacy paired with casual dating can, and often does, lead to disappointment. Now let's be clear, I'm not saying that casual dating and intimacy are bad. I am simply stating that this would be a time to proceed with extreme caution. Casual dating is important for figuring out what you like, what you don't like, and what you need in a relationship. This is a time to discover if someone else wants the same things in a relationship that you do. Most often, casual dating starts with a conversation and is followed up by the actions taken thereafter.

The art of conversation has been lost in the crossfire of social media and communication wars. We don't converse enough. It's never too early to engage in serious conversation about what you want. Asking the right questions early is what will determine if you both want the same things in a relationship. For example, discussing if you are both seeking marriage or not is a big deal. If you find common ground, that could be a key indicator to move forward full steam ahead.

It is also my belief that we must stop looking at relationships as if they're magical. It just isn't possible. Taking time to understand that you control your fate in so many ways is empowering to say the least. I, for one, am an advocate of the often dreaded *lists*. I've heard it said on so many occasions that women need to ditch their lists. Have you ever stopped to consider that you make lists for every other aspect of your life? Why would a list to reference for a mate be any less beneficial for relationships? I advocate creating a list and placing it somewhere that is visible for you to see consistently. It is a consistent reality check, and it helps to keep you grounded. I often feel that, without the lists, it is much easier to get lost in emotions when you start seeing someone. Without careful consideration of what is important to you, it could get lost in the shuffle. Most importantly, your list should not include anything that you can't be to the person that you are connected to. There is no equal distribution of love when one person asks something of another that can not be returned in kind.

No More Boyfriends

7 TIPS TO DISCOVER WHAT YOU WANT FROM A RELATIONSHIP:

1. **Look at Your Friends and the Type of People You Enjoy Being Around**
   What do your friends look like? What do you enjoy about being around them? What type of people are they?

2. **Examine Your Attributes**
   What morals, spiritual connections, and factors are you unwilling to sacrifice?

3. **Check Your Environment**
   Do you have kids? Are you single? The people, places, and things that you're around can give you a great deal of information about who you are and what you desire. What do these things say about you? What patterns can you recognize?

4. **Discover Your Love Language**
   Find out if the person that you wish to connect with can speak or identify the love language that you need and vice versa.

5. **Decide Your Goals for Your Future**

Consider your career—Do you want to be a homemaker, or work a 9-5? Each of these options will have different needs to be met.

6. **Practice Financial Fitness**
   What are your financial goals? Tolerance? How do you or your potential partner manage finances? Are there signs of financial incompatibility? This can be a big factor that hinders a relationship. Consider how they handle or spend money. How do you?

7. **Perform A Background Check**
   Examine you and your potential partner's background. Are they family oriented? Are you family oriented? Where did they come from, and does your background affect their ability to thrive in a relationship with you? Do you need healing? Do they need healing? Have they experienced past trauma? Have you experienced past trauma? All of these factors can definitely affect your relationships.

three

MEETING

*Never be too busy
to get into the
meet of things.
—T. Marie*

BEFORE YOU START to meet people make sure you're available physically and emotionally.

If you are too busy with life, your career and saving the world, do consider that this may not be a good time for you to date. Successful dating actually includes...SPENDING TIME! Yes! That's right! You can't get to know someone unless you have time to spend with them. Don't impress yourself thinking that they will be waiting for you! No ma'am, no ham, no turkey! Not going to happen!

You can't expect to find Boaz if *Yo Ass* ain't available! Don't forget, Ruth put herself in position to win! She got dolled up and put herself out there. Naomi told her to put on a cute dress and some perfume and to do something to her hair before she went out into the field. Am I the only one who interpreted the scripture that way?? LOL!

You also have to be available emotionally. If you have been hurt by a relationship of any kind whether romantic, or a friendship or family matters, there is a time for healing that is needed in order to pursue a healthy relationship. Emotionally unavailable people have a tendency to reflect their hurt, anger and bitterness onto the people who love them. In this space, they hold them responsible for the hurt that someone else has inflicted, causing collateral damage to the unsuspecting person that is attempting to be available. This viscous cycle is not fair. So before you go spreading infectious attitudes and actions with an open wound that you still have, take the time to heal and transition from being bitter to being better. Be in the right mindset to go get the love that you desire.

Now that we've got that part out of the way, let's get to the meat of things.

Where you meet someone plays a big part in the success of growing the relationship.

It's pretty true that meeting men in a club (9 times out of 9 1/2) is not going to produce what you're looking for. Most of the time, men are there just for fun, an escape, or a good ol' ego boost to show he's got it working for them. Clubs are prime for hookup scenarios, but not for a happily ever after. Granted, there are a few exceptions to this rule, but usually blending lots of alcohol and a dance floor erodes the optimum chances of a relationship.

Try venturing to your places of interest. Why? Because if you like it there and you happen to meet him there, that is an immediate connection and conversation starter. Places like museums, painting events, poetry slams, intramural team sports like softball, kickball etc., sporting events, or whatever hobby or interest you have, are great. Be adventurous. The benefit of this is valuable *me time* and an opportunity to be immersed in something you love. It would just be a bonus if you found someone to love, too. Good ol' events, whether at church or singles meeting groups are a good place to start. At least you know they are there for the possibility of genuine exchanges with people. Some other unsuspecting places are grocery stores, hardware stores, gas stations, or any places you frequet during your daily routine. What if Mr. Right was there waiting for you?

Dating sites are also very popular, and quite a few people have had successful relationships come from them.

HERE'S SOME ADVICE WHEN IT COMES TO ONLINE DATING:

You should have a video chat meeting within 48 hours. It may seem scary, but it will benefit you in the long run. This way, you can verify that they are who they say they are, connect right away, and still allow a distant introduction to each other that feels safer and easier than an in-person date.

The main thing for you to remember is that you have to be out in the world and experiencing it in order to find companionship. **Be brave. Be bold. Just go!**

ONLINE DATING TIPS

Be picky. Don't just go on a swiping or liking spree. Dating sites pay attention to your on site behavior. So if you respond to too many Men the site may read that you have no standards which causes your connection results to have more quantity and less quality.

Log on in the the dating site match reports the best time to login is between the dating site match reports the best time to login is between 8:45 a.m. and the worst times are after 11 pm. This makes plenty of sense. Most early risers or morning people are being intentional. If they have have taken time to add dating search in their morning routine, it probably means it has some importance to them and are looking for something more than casual.

When searching, swiping, or liking late at night, you are usually sifting through the guys who are looking for something far more casual or just sex.

THE FIRST 48

The chance of wasting your time is cut in half if you don't meet and greet within the first 48!! Please understand that conversation creates intimacy but conversation in person establishes a foundation on which to build. The lack of face to face conversation and engagement is one reason why it's so easy to get catfished! Words are powerful and can be persuasive but they can also leave you with hope unfulfilled. So go ahead and meet up for coffee or a quick drink. If you are not ready for a face to face, then go ahead and video chat. Let's keep it a hundred right here ladies! You need to see what you're working with in order to make a decision to move forward. All the pictures that could or could not be dated might not give you the reality of who your new potential boo is or what he looks like. What if the dating site photo is from his better days? And, no, you don't have to expect perfection, but you most definetely should be able to expect who appears on the profile.

Ghosting

Daters Beward! Ghosting can and will happen! It is a plague and a part of the game! Some men will just disappear, after you have been chatting for a while. I believe that this is due to a lack of honesty in their initial reasoning for being on the site. These guys are sometimes married, still involved and use this site to get attention or are newly broken up from a former relationship and using this site to get over someone. Consider that not everyone on dating sites are not on the site for the right reasons. Either way don't take ghosting personal, move on.

PROVE WHAT TO WHO?

When a man implies that he has to see if you are wife material and that he needs to experience wifely things from you, I call BS. You are ALREADY a wife my dear. All he needs to see is how you handle your home and business. Being a WIFE is a sacrificial exchange of power that is only meant for a man who has been INTENTIONAL about his use of your time. More importantly, he too must be willing to have the same sacrificial exchange. It is imperative that he has the capacity to appreciate who you already are.

- WHO you are is not for every man!

- WHAT you bring to the table is not for any man!
- WHEN you bring yourself to the relationship, it must be in DIVINE TIMING.
- WHERE you engage in the exchange should be a space where love is reciprocated.
- WHY you give of yourself must be confirmed his willingness to appreciate and exchange that sacrificial power with you.

Remember… if you are already a WIFE a HUSBAND will see that in you.

WHY ARE MEN OFFENDED BY WOMEN AND EMPOWERMENT?

four

Your partner's needs and desires should be compatible with yours.
— T. Marie

MEN ARE OFFENDED by women empowerment because they feel that they don't have the power role anymore in that relationship. They feel that it's causing them not to commit and doesn't allow them to be the head like they're supposed to be.

Women should look for whatever it is they need in terms of emotional support from a man and also look at who they are as a woman. It always goes back to knowing what your needs are. Every woman should look for a man that has a good moral standing and a man that values marriage and family. Your partner's desires and values should be compatible with yours. So if you want marriage, then look for someone who values marriage and has an idea of what it should look like for them. Look for morals, compatibility, and friendship because these three things will make or break a relationship.

Sometimes, men do things to deter women from empowering themselves. These men will look for a woman who has a lack. If a man is powerful or comfortable with who he is, he will look for someone who is compatible with him. But if he's not secure in who he is, he will find someone who is lacking so he can feel empowered. It makes these men feel important to convince the woman into feeling that he can be the strong role in her insecurities and weaknesses. They give the women the feeling that they can't go on without them because they convince the women that only they can fulfill her weakness. This causes the women to give these men their all. Do not ignore the red flags because that is what they want you to do.

If a man wants you to be your best, he asks you what it is that he can do to HELP you be your best. And when he is trying to help and show you how to grow more, he will do it in an encouraging and loving way, not in a discouraging and deprecating way.

7 THINGS THAT WE MUST KNOW ABOUT MEN AND SELF-HELP:

1. **Men are definitely ego-driven, regardless of how they act:** They need to be appreciated and complimented and recognized. Your words can go a long way with the way they see you. You can build up and tear down a man, which will be a factor of whether they stay in a relationship.

2. **Men are hunters:** We need to stop feeling like chasing him is a good idea (there are exceptions, but it's rare). The man is going to be the head of the house and someone who will provide and pursue you.

3. **Men are prideful** (not necessarily in a negative way): He takes pride in his accomplishments and taking care of you. He wants to be there for you.

4. **Men need to be allowed to lead:** It's in his nature to be a leader. You need to allow him to be the man. He needs the feminine side of you to soften him and let him feel things. He has his boys for being tough. You can be powerful and feminine at the SAME time!

5. **Men need their freedom:** They need time for themselves and their boys. They don't need to be with you 24 hours a day. They should be able to go out without you and be his own person outside of your relationship.

6. **Men are mirrors of their friends:** So if you meet his friends, and he comes off one way and his friends are another way, he is a mirror. If he has friends that are cheaters, or out all the time, then it's possible that he is like that as well. His counsel is important. If you can see the people he surrounds himself with, then you will see his true self.

7. **Men are adjustable:** This means that if he puts his foot down about something and that's it, he is not open to change or hearing you. You will not be heard in this kind of relationship. He needs to be adjustable—to be able to listen to other side and hear you out. You're not changing him, but he's willing to adjust his way of thinking and hear others out, otherwise, you will be the one who will be changing, not him. He needs to be able to hear and communicate well. If he can't communicate well, then you will never be heard, and he will never be able to express what he needs (like reassurance or alone time).

five
KEEPING THE PACE

Women should pace themselves for a relationship by having their own lives.

—T. Marie

UNDERSTANDING WHAT YOU want for your life before even seeking a relationship is key. Before anyone else is there, you have to be okay with yourself and who you are.

It is possible to move too fast from one relationship to the next. We use relationships as Band-Aids instead of things that complement our lives. Once you've ended a relationship, you need to evaluate why it ended, whether it was on your end or theirs, to figure out what you need to do differently. You have to make sure to get some healing and clarity before moving on to the next one.

You can often tell that you are moving too fast if you connect with the new person super quickly. That means that you have transferred feelings from the old relationship into this new relationship instead of gaining completely new feelings for them over time. Instead of taking the time to heal from the old relationship, you are just carrying over residual love to this new person, which makes it harder to get the healing that you need from the old relationship.

If there's no progression, then you may be moving too cautiously. If you're not open to this new relationship, then you may need to rethink if you want this relationship. It's unsure if moving too slow is an actual bad thing, but no one is going to wait for you if you are not willing to make progress. If you're moving too slow based on past relationships, then you probably need to do some healing before you're ready to move on to a new relationship.

Set a pace for yourself just so you can understand where you are heading and understand the goals that you have in mind. That's not just for relationships; it's for a lot of things in your life. Pacing yourself will help you grow and succeed without burning out. If you go too fast, then you'll eventually burn yourself out, but if you move too slow, then you won't ever make any progress. Pacing yourself helps you move intentionally to the goals that you have set. Everything shouldn't be calculated, but you should be moving with a purpose and goals in mind.

7 STRATEGIES TO PACE YOURSELF WHEN DATING:

1. **Have** your own life and be busy.
2. **Be** okay with who you are.
3. **Create** your own friendships and networks.
4. **Know** your end results when you're in a relationship.

5. **Seek** what you want in a person and relationship.
6. **Stop** accepting what you don't want.
7. **Accept** your shortcomings, or quirks

Know where you are. Be willing to lose to win. Be okay with losing someone good to get someone great. Too many times good is the enemy of great. We settle for fear of being lonely. And if you can't enjoy life by yourself, then you're not ready to be with anyone else anyway. If you don't like yourself, then why should he?

six

STAGES NOT TITLES

There are stages in the relationship that we must all learn to respect.

—T. Marie

EACH STAGE HAS different action levels.

The world definitely favors titles. The world teaches us to respect positions, but we choose titles over positions. Stages in life are a sign of progression and movement. Stages are more naturally progressed and a sign you have earned that position.

There are really no titles when it comes to dating. The only important titles are *husband* and *wife*. Everything else is a progression of your relationship.

Titles can help or hurt.

Help: Titles can acknowledge where you are in the relatiionship, though the only ones that are worth it are husband and wife material.

Hurt: They give you a sense of entitlement and expectation.

Stages prepare you for titles because there is a natural progression. Every stage you get to, accountability and expectations play a part. This prepares you not to move unless you're ready to go to that next stage, which means you have the power to move more intentionally. You can only expect certain things within the relationship, unless you've progressed to those stages.

Stages prepare you to move up for the ultimate goal in your relationship. It prepares you to get to the next stages within the relationship. As you move up to different stages, there are more and more things you learn to expect, and more that you learn about your significant other as well.

Knowing what each stage comes with builds our expectations. Evaluate what each stage is before you get to it. This gives you time to figure out if you want to progress to this stage and if this person is someone you want to progress with.

THE 7 STAGES OF DATING:

1. **Getting** to know the person.
2. **Presenting** your authentic self.
3. **Decide** what you want to come out of the dating situation.
4. **Finding** someone compatible.
5. **Being** available.
6. **Being** considerate and understanding who the person is.

7. **Having** the conversation about who the person is—true engagement.

Be considerate about the best dating situations. Some examples of the best dating situations are getting coffee, go for walks, bowling, or doing things that allow you to truly talk to that person. Keep in mind that expensive dates because sets up expectations that are not needed in the begining stages.

Being complete doesn't mean being good with everything that you have. You do not need someone to complete you because, if they leave, they take what you need. You may stay just to fill that need at the risk of emptying yourself.

seven
PROVE WHAT TO WHO?

There is very little benefit in proving anything to anyone.
—T. Marie

PROVE WHAT TO who? For what? Men have it bad saying, "Well, how do I know if she can be a wife if I don't experience her doing wifely things?" Sir, the same way that she had to TRUST that you can be a husband without doing husbandly things. I researched wifely and husbandly duties and check out what I found:

DUTIES OF A WIFE

A wife should listen to her husband's ideas and requests, be respectful towards him, and be eager to please him and make him happy.

A wife should be tolerant and forgiving. She shouldn't bear a grudge against him or remind him about his mistakes often. There is no quality that will endear her to her husband like the quality of tolerance and forgiveness, and there is nothing that will turn her husband against her like resentment, counting faults, and reminding him about his mistakes.

A wife, as well as the husband, should put effort in maintaining their physical beauty.

A wife should take responsibility for her husband's wealth, not spending without his permission, and being careful not to be wasteful.

Wives are expected to help her husband in dealing with the outside world, and to play her role in life by offering her opinions and advice, and supporting him in all his affairs. She never hesitates to stand by his side, encouraging him, supporting him, and offering advice and consolation.

A wife should show gratitude to her husband.

DUTIES OF A HUSBAND

The husband must give proper and sufficient sustenance/financial support to his household according to his status and means. The wife should receive full maintenance from her husband, including food, clothing, housing, education, recreation, medication, etc. Even if the wife is rich, she does not need to spend anything on her husband or household.

A husband must be kind to his wife. His behavior towards her is a measure of his faith.

He must exercise patience and should be prepared to listen to his wife's opinions in every situation. He should be open to listen to the advice of his wife in matters ranging from the smallest to the greatest.

He must treat her generously at all times. It is reportedly said: "The best gift or charity is that spent on one's wife."

He must never ever divulge the secrets of his household or marriage.

The husband should not stay away from his wife or keep his wife in a state of suspense, whether at home or abroad, for a prolonged period of time, except with her consent.

So fellas, after reading this … do you think you would give husband duties to a girlfriend? I don't think so. So why do you expect her to give her wifely duties to you before marriage? Those actions are investment, and you don't invest in anything until you've researched, found out more about it, and are pretty sure of your return.

Ladies, understand that the duties of a wife are not the duties that keep a man; it's the value he sees in you, your character, morals. He also evaluates what he needs, and if you can fulfill those needs. He can do all that without you giving yourself away. So let him. Preserve yourself.

eight
WHY DOES HE WANT TO BE WITH YOU?

If he really wants to be with you and values you, his answer will be very specific.
—T. Marie

THAT **GENERAL GENERIC** answer of, "It's just something about you," when speaking about what he values can't fly. It should be about a "filling," not a "feeling". Know the difference. Feelings are based off circumstances.

Filling is based off exchange or pouring energy, time, and effort into one another despite circumstances.

There's levels to this ISH … not TITLES.

Don't take on titles when dating. Boo, Bae, Boyfriend, and Girlfriend give a false sense of entitlement without a true commitment. As women, we have a tendency to commit on wife level in a boyfriend situation because by nature, once something is "ours," we want to take care of it. We go above and beyond the level we are actually in. Commit on the level that he commits to you. Don't over commit yourself to a situation where you don't have the same return.

> **Dating:** Spending time, getting to know each other, discovery stage. Is this someone I can see myself spending/sharing time with?
>
> **Intentional:** Intentional is what you might want to call the gf/bf stage. The title is not there yet, but you have the intention.
>
> **Engaged:** The promise to fully commit—the preparation for Marriage.

Marriage: Full commitment, the becoming of ONE.

WHY DOES HE WANT YOU?

Knowing that a man is interested in you is important. Considering why he is interested is just as important. This answer will most often be based on his value system and the things that he needs to fulfill them. Do not be confused in thinking that his interest in you is about your value system, it is not. I know I know! You're a bad chick. I mean, look at you! You take care of your business, your household is on point, your body is on point, you smell good, you can cook, you still have your edges, and all that good stuff right? In your mind you are a cold catch! And you are for the one who's interested in that.

Be warned, all men are not fulfilled by the same things. It is possible that you may have all the right things in the eyes of one person but appear to be lacking in the eyes of another. This is where you must decipher the difference between random dating and dating with strategy and purpose.

Consider the following questions: What are his interests? What are his values? What does he feel about family or women with children? The things that are important to him serve as the determining factors as to whether or not he commits to you or wastes your time until he finds the one that fits his requirements.

Yes ma'am!! He WILL WASTE YOUR TIME!! He will do what you allow him to do with your mind, body, spirit and resources until what he wants comes along. That's why it's up to you to know why he wants to be with you. If by chance he's not specific, then be very cautious. You would never be woman enough to convince him that you are the one when his mind and interests deem that you are not.

nine

CHESS, NOT CHECKERS

Finding a man is not the hard part, keeping one is a different conversation.
—T. Marie

SLOW DOWN SPEED racer! We have a tendency to move so fast because we get addicted to that "NEW CAR SMELL". Ya know, you get something new and everything seems good, but you really have not experienced it enough to know how it actually feels. We as women always want our king, but what we don't realize is what it takes to get it, and the responsibility that comes with keeping him. Like in chess, your moves must be very intentional and thought out.

To win, you have to make the right moves ... and knowing which moves to make comes with insight and knowledge from lessons learned along the way. So when you get that king to join you in the game, remember he is the head (most important piece on the board) but YOU, QUEEN, are the most POWERFUL! Not only do you make more moves, but you protect the KING! So make sure you're properly prepared for the task. Take your time getting there and enjoy the ride.

Checkers is about how fast you play the game and chess is about how strategically you play the game. It takes more strategy and patience in chess. In the game of chess, the queen is the most important part of the game.

If you're settling for what you can get at that time, you're just playing a checker game. Like in dating, if you're out there to just date with no strategy, then you're just accepting how the game goes and accepting however it ends up. There's no strategy or intention besides recreation.

Playing with strategy, you have to know the chess game and know what the end result will be. You have to be intentional and directional.

Playing checkers gets you familiar with the board. If you're not ready for that stage, playing checkers prepares you and gives you foresight on what it looks like and how it's played Checker-like dating will help you get familiar with the dating game. This approach has similar factors to the strategic approach, but it could hinder you by giving you a false sense of how to win in the long run.

Playing chess, you know what it takes to get to the end goal of your strategy. You may use the strategies too early in your dating process. You may strategize on someone who may not be ready and who is still playing checkers. You just have to realize when it's time to play chess and when it's time to play checkers. And that will obviously depend on each person.

7 WAYS THAT WE PLAY CHECKERS WHEN DATING:

1. **We don't find out what the person's end result looks like:** You've dated and gone out, but you haven't talked about what your intentions for the future are.

2. **You don't take what you want seriously**

3. **Not having a clear understanding of what your deal breakers are**

4. **Not having a life of your own or your own things going on**

5. **Wasting Time:** Hoping that someone will become the person that you want if you just keep staying with them.

6. **Being okay with you:** When you're not okay with yourself, then you are just trying to find someone that fills spaces, which means you'll accept anything that will fill your spaces.

7. **Entertaining Men with No End in Mind:** When we entertain men who don't have the same reciprocation when they know what our intentions and end goals are.

ten
INTENTION VS. INTENTIONAL

*No matter what intentions he expresses, his **actions** will show if he is intentional.*

—T. Marie

A MAN WHO WANTS to be with you moves past intentions and becomes intentional.

INTENTION: a thing intended; an aim or plan.
synonyms:
  intent, meaning: premeditation, forethought, preplanning

INTENTIONAL: done on purpose; deliberate.
synonyms:
deliberate, calculated, conscious, planned, meant, studied, knowing, willful, purposeful, purposive, done on purpose, premeditated, preplanned, preconceived.

We all have good intentions. Our intentions are like setting up a plan; it's a list of things that you want to do. Being intentional is following through the plan with actions. Good intentions do not always mean that the person is intentional.

Women should look for the action behind the words that a man says. The best man could have the best intentions, but does he also have time to put in the work for what it takes to pursue and have a relationship with you? Everything that a person wants, they have time for.

Anything a man really wants to do, he does it intentionally. Like losing weight or striving for a good career ... the same goes for you! If he wants you, he will be very intentional about pursuing you. Anything that anybody wants to happen, they do it with intention and they become intentional. Intentions are words, but being intentional is action.

A man is intentional because his actions will line up with what you need from him. When in a relationship, you usually let that person know what you need. It's important to know what those things are and relay them to your partner. In turn, the person must decide if it's something that they can/cannot do and if it's something that they want/don't want to do. If they're truly intentional, then they can and want to do those things for you.

7 CONSIDERATIONS REGARDING MEN AND INTENTION

1. **Take note of a man's character:** Character is so important when dating because it can decide what they can/cannot do and what they will/will not do.

2. **If he's self-centered/selfish:** It's hard for these types of people to focus on other people. Everything will be about him and what he wants, instead of what's best for the other person.

3. **Is he an action person, or is he just a big talker?** It's important to date people for a bit in order to decipher if they're going to be good at actually following through with their intentions or not.

4. **Does he have goals for himself?** Asking what kind of goals and plans he has for himself is a good way to decipher if he's intentional. If he has goals outside of the relationship, then that is promising.

5. **Intentional people tend to be givers rather than takers:** You have to see how they are with the people around them. Do they have the character of leaving their mark and leaving things

better than the way they found them? It's very hard to be a taker and be intentional at the same time.

6. **Look at the people they surround themselves with**: Usually, the people they surround themselves with will give you a good idea about the character that they have. You want them to have a supportive group of friends that will also call them out if they are on the wrong path.

7. **The way they approach you**: A man approaching to date should have a goal in mind. They're not looking for just anything; they are looking for a specific type of person because they have a goal in mind. They are not trying to waste time because they value it.

eleven

DETOUR

We should embrace detours.
—T. Marie

A DETOUR IN DATING happens when you find ways to get around the unnecessary stuff. These are tools and advice that you can use to avoid the long route, like Waze for our vehicles.

No matter what intentions he expresses, his ACTIONS will show if he is intentional. Detours have a significant purpose. They are there to reroute you when you're either in a situation too long, or to keep us from experiencing something we don't need. It helps to look at detours as a way to reroute you in a healthy way.

Expect that they may happen. We have to be open to them and realize that they're going to show us a new way. If we don't keep our minds open, then we can be disappointed when things don't go the way we're used to or expect to.

They can impact our ability to love. They can be frustrating. They move us from our timeline or bring us away from something that we are expecting we want. That's why it helps to keep an open mind.

Do not take them personally. Nothing is wrong with you. We should take them as a blessing or an assistance. Detours will enlighten you and allow you to make necessary adjustments.

You will learn that there is always more than one way to navigate a relationship, and we have to look at the person that we are dealing with, and the person that we have become. You can learn patience with yourself and others. It can also help you gain a sense of discernment within yourself and other people. You can also learn to avoid certain detours by learning what you want.

A way to predict an oncoming detour is to know the route you want to take and knowing what you want. For example, if you want a relationship, detours will show you to avoid the people that don't want relationships. Or if you're a faith-based woman, then you won't deal with a man who isn't faith-based or of a different faith.

You can be your own detour. We have the power to establish one based on our thoughts and feelings in a relationship. This is what happens when we don't know what we want. When we do know and understand what we want, we make better decisions and judgements and you use wisdom in those decisions. A lot of times when we don't know what we want, we try to change the route that we are on and it doesn't work.

When there's a stall, when you seem to be in the same place, or when you are constantly moving in opposite directions is when a detour is needed. A stall is a good one because if you're going in one direction and you stop completely, then you definitely need a detour.

twelve
LOVE LANGUAGE

Men say a lot of things but actions will always speak louder than words.

—T. Marie

LOVE LANGUAGES ARE displayed in many ways. One of the most important parts of dating on purpose is to know your internal love language as well as that of the person you're dating. The next step would be to see if you are built to accept the way the person that you are dating communicates and vice versa.

We know that actions speak louder than words and if a man wants you, he will show you but what we don't always know is what that particular person's actions look like. If you are dating or even thinking of dating, one of the first things that you should do is take The Five Love Language test (https://www.5lovelanguages.com). I also recommend taking a personality test to find out about who you are before getting into a relationship.

One of my favorite personality tests is called the Myers-Briggs Test.[1] This test helps you understand what makes you tick and how you relate to others as well as how to benefit from that knowledge in your everyday life.

After learning a little bit more about yourself, you are empowered to better express your needs to your mate, while understanding how to make them feel loved as well.

---

1 www.mbtionline.com

The Five Love Languages:

1. Words of Affirmation
2. Acts of Service
3. Receiving Gifts
4. Quality time
5. Physical Touch

Now there are going to be some things that a man will show you to let you know that he's in it for the long haul.

When you have a man who can communicate effectively, that you are compatible with and follows up with these actions, trust and believe that you are on your way to something great.

If he wants you, his actions will show it.

He Listen To You: With attention and recalls what you said.

He Shows His Vulnerability: Opens up about his dreams, fears, desires, and weaknesses because he feels he can trust you.

He Loves How You Look On Your Worst Days: He makes you feel beautiful no matter what.

He Is Proud Of You/Supports you/Invests in you: Nothing is more important to a man than his time and his money. When he puts these things in to you, he's truly feeling you.

He Sticks Up For You: Can't nobody say nothing about you, his momma, his sister, his friend—NOBODY. He might even come and step to your boss if he's giving you a hard time.

He Makes Sacrifices For You: Going without, putting you and your needs before his. This is, to me, the LOUDEST way that a man can show you he loves you.

thirteen
EXPECTATIONS AND CREDENTIALS

Never under any circumstances allow men to make you feel that you should have no expectations.

—T. Marie

THE WHOLE JUST let it flow and see where it goes is not always the answer, especially when they have expectations for you and—believe me—they do.

It's okay to have standards, and it's okay to know what you want from a man, in a man, and from your relationship. But mind you … the longer your checklist, the shorter your mate list. Make your filters make sense.

Expectation: You should expect people to live up to their word, their character, and their commitment. You should know what they expect from you when it comes to certain things like running a household, their take on money, and raising kids. This is vital information when deciding to take on someone as a life partner.

Credentials: What kind of relationship does he have with his parents/family/kids? What kinds of friends does he have? Does he love the Lord? What were his example of love? What type of environment did he grow up in? Can he fight, or do I have to take up for him? LOL! In the words of TK Kirkland, "Who raised you?"

You can't have permanent expectation in a temporary situation, so know where you are in that situation with that person.

EXPECTATIONS IN CREDENTIALS

Let's talk about expectations a little bit. People are quick to say that you should have little to no expectations because it's a setup for disappointment. Where that may be true, in relation to the way that you give or serve without expectation of anything in return, it makes absolutely no sense when it comes to creating relationships. Setting expectations is not asking for perfection, but it is asking that you take care of the roles and duties for the position that you chose to play and that you live up to the standards of that position. If he says he wants to love you, then it is ok to expect that he loves you. If he says that he is going to be there for you, then it is acceptable to expect that he be there for you. If he says that he is going to wash your car, then dammit it is acceptable for you to expect him to wash your car! LOL! You should expect him to do what he says he is going to do. Otherwise why have him? Now this doesn't mean that f he makes a mistake and doesn't come through a time or two to throw away the whole bowl of fruit, but what I AM saying is that if he can't live up to who he says he is or who he wants to be in your life, then yeah... toss out the fruit and the package it came in.

Credentials are important as well. Don't be afraid to ask him about his credentials for the role that you want him to play in your life. Ask about his previous experience. You need and deserve to know his backstory.

Trust and believe how he was taught to play, will tell you a lot about his game.

fourteen
MEN TO AVOID

The problem is that women think he will change. He won't. The mistake men make is thinking she'll never leave. She will.

—T. Marie

THERE IS SOMETHING in our ego that makes us feel like we have the power to change a man.

No More Boyfriends

That doctrine that Steve Harvey and other men speak about that the right woman can change a man is B.S. Even after having this conversation with men I have come to discover that it is not always about the right woman, it's about the right timing! There are times when the right woman, a good woman, a wifely woman, a faithful woman will serve as the starter kit for a man because either he wasn't ready or he really wasn't ready!

You can never be good enough for a man who is not ready to commit or a man who doesn't want you. We have to stop thinking that we can change a man's mind and start understanding that we have the power to change the man we choose.

All things considered, let's talk about the type of men to avoid.

The Blamer

Nothing is ever his fault. Every failed relationship, every missed opportunity, everything that didn't go right is because of someone or something else. There is no accountability with this guy and he will always be the victim. He gets in his feelings when you mention how something he did affected you and instead of addressing that issue, he turns the table and says "Well what about you when you blah blah blah blah blah." You will find yourself exhausted trying to get him to understand how you feel. Don't exhaust yourself or stick around to try to help him see the light.

The Show Off

This is the guy who has to have the best of everything and let people know it. His identity is in his work, his money, his looks and his possessions. In reality there's really an underlying self-esteem issue. The things that he has are the things that make him who he is. That is how he identifies your value as well and if you lose any of those things or if any of those things change so will his interest in you. Remember, how he's seen by others is important to him. Often, the value that he places on you not only comes from how he sees you but how others view you. There's no room for error with this guy.

THE ATTENTION SEEKER

This guy lacks self-esteem and is looking for validation in any form he can get it. He is easily swayed because he is rarely fulfilled or satisfied. He will seek attention from someone else. This has nothing to do with you and everything to do with him. He is the guy who needs to know that he still has it and is willing to leave a crack in the door of his relationship to anything outside factor that will boost his self-esteem. He's the guy that post pictures on social media with his shirt off, showing his abs, posts pictures of his new car, or brags about the people he knows. He thrives on seducing others into wanting him and working hard to get people to like him. Getting attention means more to him than how his behavior affects his relationship with you. This guy cares more about getting his feel of attention than how his behavior makes you feel.

THE FOLLOWER

Webster describes follower someone who… is guided by another person or by a group but the Uban Dictionary hits a little harder.

1. Rather than decide what's right for them, will adopt the beliefs and opinions of another (or others).
2. When they are in a group, they will adopt the belief systems, attitudes, and values of others in the group.
3. In a case where they might move from hanging around one group to another, they will completely change their attitudes, values, etc. and adopt the ones of the new group.

These are just a few of the reasons why followers do not make good mates. Their decisions are based on the opinions of others more than their own. They are easily influenced and afraid to take a risk. They lack a strong, independent mind, and self-confidence and they are easily swayed, which also demonstrates a lack of emotional intelligence. These guys are easily distracted by their surroundings and lack the ability to anchor themselves in long-term relationships.

All it takes is for someone that they are influenced by to doubt their relationship or the girl that they're seeing for problems to arise. Instead of being strong enough to stand in their own feelings, thoughts and opinions, they will take a second look and become fixated on the person that influences the way they think. Which leads me to the next guy you should definitely avoid...

A Man with Bad Friends!!!

Show me a man's friends and I'll show you who he really is! You are who you hang out with. A man's friends or lack thereof can reveal a great deal about his character. Remember, people can only be around what they can tolerate or are in agreeance with. If he has friends that cheat, lie, and have no spiritual guidance, then you would be hard pressed to not eventually discover these same qualities in him.

Your Tango has a great article that is worth checking out, 12 Things You Can Learn About Your Man Just by Looking at His Friends.[2]

And if he doesn't have any friends that means he relies fully on his own opinions, feelings and emotions, which are biased because he is only consulting himself. A man who has no council, has no direction. He's being led by what makes him feel good at the moment and he can turn that moment into a life-time decision.

There's nothing wrong with judging someone by their entourage. His friends contribute to his life in a major way. Decide accordingly.

---

2 https://www.yourtango.com/2017305588/what-his-friends-can-tell-you-about-him-just-looking-them

Bonus: LET'S TALK ABOUT SEX

We think we want sex, but the truth is that it is not always sex. Most often, it's intimacy you want. To be touched, looked at, and it mixed.

—T. Marie

WOMEN SHOULD GET away from the idea that they can have sex and not get attached, 'cause 9 out of 10 times, we do, while men can just have sex and not form any connection at all. It's chemically impossible for women not to form an attachment while having casual sex. Mixing casual sex and dating is dangerous when trying to intentionally date.

The biggest trap is the scenario where the man tries to convince the women by saying that they're both adults. Do not fall for the trap. Don't set yourself up to get into a position that would create the opportunity to have sex if you're not ready for it.

In a sense, it can help by showing you what you're getting into. It will also depend on the type of person you are, and if it is actually important to you. However, if you're dating someone and you become attached because of sex, but he hasn't connected the same way then, it can really hurt you.

7 WAYS THAT WOMEN CAN PROTECT THEIR FEELINGS REGARDING SEX AND DATING

1. **Don't do it:** Give yourself time to understand what that means for you.

2. **Really understand what that connection means to you:** Figure out if you can disconnect from the casualness.

3. **Talk to him about what the idea of sex means to him:** If you decide to do it, see how the guy feels about it. Most people who are quick to move sexually don't value it as much

4. **Don't use your sex as a reward:** Don't try to make him think that your sex is a prize. Don't go in thinking that you are gonna get him to stay and commit by giving him sex.

5. **Make sure that he's not taking you and the sex you're giving for granted:** If you're going to do it, make sure that you have connected with him enough that he cares about you.

6. **Self gratification - Are you craving just sex?** Or are you craving the intimacy and attention of someone? If it's the latter, then you want more then just sex, which means that you'll eventually develop feelings for the perosn that you are casually having sex with.

7. **Consult your counsel:** Use your friends or a trusted person to talk to about how you're feeling and thinking. Explore what your goals are in regards to dating and in regards to the role sex can play in your goals.

No More Boyfriends

p.s.
WHOSE IS IT?

Smile that. Laugh with someone. Feel safe. Feel like someone's really got you. That's what we crave.
—T. Marie

NOW THIS HAS gotta be the most ridiculous, narcissist question anyone can ask during sex!

Whenever I'm asked during the moment, it almost makes me laugh, especially when he's not really bringing it like that …

But you gotta really ask yourself in real life though … Whose. Is. It? You gotta ask this waaaaaaaaaaay before you give it away because to be honest, once you do, you can't get it back. Now it's his, and the last guy you were in a situationship with, and the other guy you had a friends with benefits with ... and oh, dont forget that other guy you kinda just slipped under because you were in the mood ... AND that stupid ex that you got the, "Hey big head" text from because he missed you. Or was it because he missed IT? Either way, he hit IT, and now you regret IT.

Now, I ain't tryna tell you what to do with IT, but you gotta understand ITS value and what IT was created for. Let's start by giving IT a name: We'll call her "TREASURE".

noun: treasure
    1. a quantity of precious metals, gems, or other valuable objects
    2. a very valuable object
~informal
a person whom the speaker loves or who is valued for the assistance they can give.

verb: treasure; 3rd person present: treasures; past tense: treasured; past participle: treasured; gerund or present participle:

treasuring
1. keep carefully (a valuable or valued item).
Synonyms: cherish, hold dear, prize, value greatly; adore, dote on, love, be devoted to, worship
2. value highly.

Funny how naming something—branding it, if you will—changes the way you see it. It's no longer just a stray; it's a part of the family and has value. And the way you take care of it is different because of the ways you see it …

Most times, we name things to give them value and the names reflects its value. Whether it's a baby named Mercedes because that mama or daddy liked top of the line things and wanted that child to always remember her value, or Micah which means "Godlike" and want her to give power and her strength in her Creator. We name it to reflect not only its importance, but also how WE see it!!

So if you were asked, "Whose TREASURE is this?" You might not only answer that question differently, but when you ask yourself, you'll also value it differently and be less likely to give it to just anyone.

You gotta understand the power of sex and why it was created. To be honest, it's the strongest narcotic that God ever created … and it was not for casual use!

In the act of sex, a man and a women become one flesh.[3]

Biophysics has caught up with the Bible. When a man and a woman are together in a sex act, a chemical reaction happens in the human brain that has the same effect as heroin—which is very addictive. This means that a man and a woman, when together, become connected on a deep level.

This is why you can't have casual sex. It doesn't exist.

This is why you get addicted to porn.

---

3 http://gospelrelevance.com/2012/01/12/mark-driscoll-6-reasons-why-god-created-sex-for-marriage/)

Even men who frequent prostitutes usually frequent the same one over and over and over. They are physically connected to them.

If you're into your spouse and your spouse is into you, by the grace of God, you will become into them and physically connected to them, desiring them. You will become one flesh, one family, one bed to glorify the one God.

God built our bodies to connect with our spouse during sex.

When we connect with anything else, it leads to death. But we can repent and be made clean and connect with our spouse.[4]

God created sex and marriage. He created both for the purpose of love.

(And I believe he created it so POWERFULLY so you you would continue to yearn for each other.)

---

4 Reference https://www.ucg.org/the-good-news/sex-is-intended-for-pleasure

The former should be reserved for and experienced only in the latter. When this happens, sex and love become the blessing that God intended them to be.

Though the English word *sex* is not found in the Bible, the Bible is prolific with references to sexuality. Some references show that harmful consequences result from sex's misuse, but many others illustrate that God created sex to provide exquisite pleasure for married couples.

Notice these words of instruction to a young man: "Drink water from your own well—share your love only with your wife. Why spill the water of your springs in public, having sex with just anyone? You should reserve it for yourselves. Don't share it with strangers. Let your wife be a fountain of blessing for you. Rejoice in the wife of your youth … Let her breasts satisfy you always. May you always be captivated by her love."[5]

The Song of Solomon is a joyous account that uses poetic language to romantically describe sexual interaction and the endearing words

---

5 Proverbs 5:15-19, New Living Translation

exchanged between devoted mates and includes a tasteful description of the sex act itself.

Some have wondered why this book about physical love should be in the Bible. It does not expound religious themes, and it contains no obvious references to God. Yet it is most appropriate to include in the Bible a love story that shows how sexual relations should be, in view of the fact that "history began with a wedding[6] and will climax with the Marriage Supper of the Lamb." [7]

Just because you use it differently, doesn't mean the strength of its addiction or the side effects changes. A drug is still a drug and when used as directed, it can create amazing results, even healing (cause yaaassss baby with the right one, it feels soooo AMAZING).

So use as prescribed. The best is in the confines of a marriage but, at the very least, with someone you know also recognizes not only its value, but yours too.

....

    6 Genesis 2:18-25, ibid.
    7 Revelation 19:6-10, ibid.

SIDE NOTE: I believe in self pleasuring. If you feel like you just need to get one off, take care of yourself … especially before you go out with someone … lol. If self pleasuring doesn't do it for you, and you need to be touched, that's usually an indicator that the desire you have is more than sexual, but for intimacy. Be careful because when you confuse the two, that can be a self set up.

Choose to fulfill your own desires in many ways, so when it's time, you're already filled. You're just looking to complement … like a good accessory should … lol. Ya know, you're already dressed, but when you add a hot pump, earrings, and that bangin' clutch, oh baby … watch out world! When you got on a good outfit, you wouldn't just add any old accessories, would ya? Add those that bring out what you already got.

#accessorizewell

#beChosenWisely

OUTRO

And suddenly that faithful, loyal, loving, God chasing man you've been praying for will find you.
—T. Marie

IT ALSO DEPENDS on the best you that you can be. The most important part of being in a solid relationship is being a solid woman. Understanding what your flaws are, understanding what you want and who you are, helps keep you from falling into a pattern of falling into relationships that cause hurt or don't produce anything healthy. Knowing yourself helps you avoid those painful paths and find things that will make you happy.

Now that you readers have this information, use it as a guide when you start dating. It's definitely something that you should read before you jump into the dating game. When I started writing this, I realized that the things in this book could have helped me to do things differently. This supplies instruction on what to present in the dating game and what you should want or look for in a relationship. It's all about being solid before you start.

My vision is that women will not feel like they have to go through all this brokenness to get into a relationship and find love. Love is not a reward that you have to win or battle for. Love is a gift from someone who has seen your value and wants to give it to you. We can't look at love like a reward because God gave us love freely, so we should take that same idea into relationships. And Love in a relationship is different from the Love in marriage.

Katrina Marie Curtis

The greatest lesson that I have learned is that I am good enough. Women seem to think that they don't deserve love because of multiple reasons. But I learned that I am good enough, and whoever loves me will love every part of me. I don't have to change a thing to get them to love me. And it's not that we are never enough; we just may be with the wrong person and sometimes, that can make us feel like we are not enough. But we are.

I serve on a panel called *The Conversation* which is a relationship conversation that everyone should be having about stabilizing for the family. It's important for me to help men and women figure out how to stabilize relationships and get rid of the ideas that TV and movies give. It's something that I feel called to do. I want to carry *The Conversation* nationwide.

Women can get involved by taking a step back and understanding what it means to be a woman. We have to be everything sometimes and when that happens, we lose our feminine energy and become a certain way when we meet men. We have to remember that a man wants a feminine woman. I don't mean a weak women, but a feminine one. We have to learn to take off our many hats and just be a woman when you're at home with him.

I will never stop fighting for the way we visualize each other as black men and black women. It's sad the way that music has influenced young women to feel like they have to be and dress a certain way and how boys view women now. Women and men need to realize the value that women have, especially in regards to how women are treated in relationships. Especially in the black community. If you listen to the music in the black community and see how different it is in the white community, then you see how young men are influenced to treat women and how young girls are influenced to act and dress.

Say What!
QUOTES WORTH KEEPING FROM NO MORE BOYFRIENDS

//

Don't love too deeply until you're sure that person loves you with the same depth. The depth of your love today can be the depth of your wounds tomorrow.

//

If you are not ready or willing to be held accountable for your behavior, you are not ready for a healthy relationship.

No More Boyfriends

//

My last relationship taught me not to ignore signs or my gut feelings. I learned how to love myself and not to put anyone above my happiness or my dreams. I now know my worth. I know what I want, and won't settle for less again. I have no regrets. I needed to learn those lessons."

//

When you love yourself first, it gives people the option to love you correctly or leave you the hell alone."

//

I like being alone but I want to have someone to be alone with."

"Be ye busy but available."

"Make room for people who want to love you."

"If I am empowering myself to choose differently in search of fulfilling relationships, it doesn't make me bitter, it makes me better."

"Baby you can do it, take your time, do it right."

"Men want love, support, affection, hot meals, raw sex, and commitment... but only as friends."

No More Boyfriends

"You are the desire of your future husband's heart."

"A man knows who his heart belongs to. You can cook his food and do backflips on his well you know. . . but if his heart has not chosen you, then it will never be you."

"The strategy to find love can still be romantic, just use both your head and your heart."

"Never forget that if a person wants to do something, they will find a way to do it. The same sentiment rings true if they don't."

Katrina Marie Curtis

//

If someone wants to just go with the flow, beware, they preparing to waste your time."

//

May you attract someone who speaks your love language so you don't spend a lifetime translating your soul."

//

You can't be interested in inconsistent."

//

Carefully observe the habits of a man who wants to get close to you. His words are valuable but his habits are who he proves himself to be."

//

The man you choose to be your life partner will affect everything in your life. Your mental health, your peace of mind, the love inside you, your happiness, how you get through tragedies, your success, how your children are raised, will all be impacted! Choose wisely. "

//

We think we want sex, but the truth is that it is not always sex. Most often, it's intimacy you want. To be touched, looked at, and it mired."

//

Smile that. Laugh with someone. Feel safe. Feel like someone's really got you. That's what we crave."

And suddenly that faithful, loyal, loving, God chasing man you've been praying for will find you.

About
KATRINA T'MARIE CURTIS

Media Personality

Relationship Advocate

Author

KATRINA T'MARIE CURTIS is one of Atlanta's most notable beauty, news and entertainment personality. Carrying a degree in media broadcasting from the Connecticut School of Broadcasting and a certification in Cosmetology, T'Marie is known as Atlanta's QUEEN OF TALK, using her down home charm and tough life experiences to inform uplift and provide women with the skills they need to achieve success and confidence the fit and FAB way!

T'Marie has produced shows for many major on-air talents and her voice has filled the airways for several years. Throughout her career, she's interviewed with the likes of Mona Scott Young, Lynn Whitfield, Kenny Lattimore, and KeKe Wyatt to name a few, but for the last three years, her love to inform and entertain has shown through on her nationally syndicated radio show, "It's T'Marie," which currently broadcasts on Power 108.9.

T'Marie's passion for beauty and media started young. She grew up in the small town of Hickman, Kentucky, with a yearning to entertain boiling in her blood. She quickly realized her energetic spirit and fierce work ethic were destined for a bigger city, so she packed up her two-year-old daughter and took her skills as a master stylist to Atlanta. After divorce stripped her mentally spirituality and financially. With her strength and faith in God, she was able to transform her life experiences into teachable moments for others and draw audiences far and wide.

Both the success and challenges of dating post divorce lead T'Marie to write the book "NO MORE BOYFRIENDS". She has garnered the attention of many women with her catchphrase: No More Boyfriends. As love and fate would have it, the phrase morphed into an online community that shares tips for fearless dating and falling in love on your own terms. In her, candidly inspiring book, T. Marie exposes the lies and misconceptions that far too often hinder us from living in the abundance of self-love, lies that many of us have adopted as our truths when it comes to love and marriage.

The book uncrates the misconceptions of personal experiences that left her feeling unworthy of true love and reveals practical strategies to unravel the greatest love of all.

With gifted hands, open heart and transparency, T'Marie plans to maximize her ability to pour into others by using her nonprofit Blessed Tresses, an organization that teaches women how to beautify from the inside out, also by continuing to speak into others over the radio and in her newest role as a relationship advocate. Her passion is to equip women with the tools, wisdom and accountability to create love and life that they desire. Her ultimate goal: to help create relationships that lead to families who build communities that produce, provide and THRIVE!! T'Marie states "It's time with live life on PURPOSE in PURPOSE"!

T. Marie on Social Media

FacebookKatrina TMarie Curtis /No More Boyfriends Group

Instagram ....@tmarie4u @_nomoreboyfriends

Twitter..@tmarie4u

LinkedIn ....Katrina TMarie Curtis

Website ....itstmarie.com nomoreboyfriends.com

Email...contactitstmarie@gmail.com

www.ingramcontent.com/pod-product-compliance
Lightning Source LLC
Chambersburg PA
CBHW051418070526
44584CB00023B/3477